Permission

I0177340

SUSAN UTTER

ISBN:978-1-7358918-0-4

DEDICATION

To those who dream but cannot do and everyone else

CONTENTS

ACKNOWLEDGEMENTS

There are literally tons of books offering advice on loving yourself, success, and fulfillment. This short, small book, addresses all that from one single perspective: permission.

Without realizing it I've been on a permission journey most of my life. As I sit today in my San Francisco office a memory surfaces: It's 1994 and I'm holding a numbered plate, chin-level while my picture is taken. I pipe up in my perky voice, "Wow! This is just like what you do with real criminals!".

The photo captures the moment when I realize I am the criminal. How did I get to this nice office from that regrettable photo-op in 1994? That's the journey of this book.

I've arrived at many dead ends in my life – places where the walls were too high to climb and too thick to break down. Time and time and again the way over the walls, hidden at first, was permission.

I had to give myself permission to get past the walls to the freedom on the other side. As I completed my permission lessons my internal garden grew. The garden is now budding, buzzing, and bearing fruit. Fruit that nourishes and sends out tendrils of hope, one of which looks just like this book in your hands..

"We accept the Love we think we deserve."Stephen Chbosky

1
MOTHERS

I used to refer to myself as a motherless child. I felt absolutely desolate. This led to very sad thoughts which I internalized. I decided there must be something wrong with me. Around age four I started wondering "Why did my mommy leave?". I remember asking my parent if I was an ugly baby. I was trying to find out what was wrong with me.

As I sit here at the ripe age of 58, writing out my journey from inherent wrongness to wholly loved, I got to thinking about mothers, specifically the Hallmark version of mothers. After many years of self-inquiry, therapy and study, I have come to realize that although I didn't start out with Hallmark mothers, I did find some along the way.

Incubator Mom

Incubator Mom is the name I've given to my biological mom, the one I grew inside. She left when I was 18 months old so I don't know much about her. What I do know is this.

She was probably only sixteen or seventeen when she got married.   She was then told by relatives to have a child quickly so the marriage couldn't be annulled.   My older brother was born in no time and I was conceived when he was just nine months old. Would you choose to be changing diapers while enduring morning sickness? At age nineteen?

Knowing this little of her story has given me the opportunity to have compassion and empathy for both her and myself. If I ever get a chance to meet her, I'll give her a hug and tell her it must've been so hard to leave two babies. I fervently hope she's found happiness.

Pushy Scary Mom

The second mother I had was sadistic. I ended up with her when my remaining parent was drafted into the Vietnam War. I was with her up to age four and details are sketchy.

I do remember being made to stand still, naked, holding onto the table edge, while she pushed me. Then she'd hit me for moving. She wanted me to call her mother, but I was confused because I already had a mother who had mysteriously disappeared. I didn't want to call this scary woman mother and this made her even angrier.

Although I didn't remember these bad experiences until later in life, * I do find it interesting that I never took my baby girl over to visit Pushy Scary — despite living minutes apart!

Pushy Scary is dead now and has been for many years. From her I learned not to trust. This is the lesson I carried with me into the next mother relationship.

*Years later, in college psychology classes, I learned that early physical, sexual or emotional abuse can result in symptoms of drug addiction, chronic insomnia, many sexual partners, early sexual encounters, and an inability to form lasting intimate relationships. My life is decorated with these symptoms.

Off to a Bad Start Mom

When I met Off to a Bad Start as a four-year-old, I was told she would be my new mommy. She wanted to love me, and put her little girl in sweet dresses but things did not go well.

Photos from these days show me wearing lovely dresses and a manic smile. The more she reached out the more I retreated. The child psychiatrist who was called in to help incorrectly pointed the finger of blame at Off to a Bad Start. This certainly didn't help us get along any better!

She had done nothing but love me the best she could. She was only 15 or 16 years older than me, what tools could she have had to use on a traumatized little girl?

Despite her good intentions we never recovered from that bad start.

Like two hard of hearing people trying to communicate without their hearing aids we just couldn't hear what the other had to say. Over the twelve years in this misshapen relationship my maladjustments took firm hold and solidified into a cement barrier.

Tom's Mom

A neighborhood mother with a toddler named Tom gave me my first babysitting assignment. She was the first person outside of my household to give me responsibility and this allowed me to earn money. Money I could spend on candy! Tom's mom appreciated my help and introduced me to her neighbor, Little Vicky's' mom. My first recommendation! The introduction to Little Vicky's mom had a very positive impact on my life and I send gratitude Tom's Mom.

Little Vicky's Mom

I loved hanging out with this family. Little Vicky's Mom was so kind to me. At first, she didn't know about my home life -- that I was sneaking out and lying about things. She didn't know I cleaned my room by shoving everything into the closet or under my bed. No, Little Vicky's Mom thought I was wonderful.

She taught me how to make Key Lime Pie out of frozen limeade, sweetened condensed milk, and a ready-made graham cracker pie crust. I loved her so much. In time, she came to know about the difficulties in my home. After I ran away and was placed in foster care, Little Vicky's mom and her husband offered to become foster parents thereby releasing me from ward of the state status. I wanted to live with this family desperately! But Off to a Bad

Start and my father would not allow it so I stayed in the system.

I lost contact with Little Vicky's family shortly after they moved out of state. Little Vicky's Mom, if you're reading this book, please know I love you. Thank you for teaching me hope.

The Divorcee

I also babysat for a divorcee. She dressed quite glamorously when she went on dates. I remember watching her get ready and I can still smell the powders and perfume.

Now that I'm older I understand the false cheer she put on along with her lipstick as hopes for a new start for her and her son blossomed anew with each date. She kindly let me live with her for a few short months in my difficult sixteenth year. Unfortunately, during that time we were victims of a violent crime that appears elsewhere in this book. Two weeks after the crime I moved to California and we never spoke again.

Mark's Mom

I met Mark's mom soon after I moved to California.   She had a sweet spirit and I always wished I was a tiny girl who could fit in her lap.

When my own tiny girl was born, Mark's mom filled an empty grandmother role. She and her husband traveled several hundred miles to bring smiles and sun suits with matching bonnets for my baby girl. Eventually there were no more visits. (Keeping connected to people wasn't my strong suit then.) But in my mind's eye I can still see her smile, and I enjoy seeing the photographs of my baby girl kitted out so fashionably.

Mark's Mom showed me that mothers could be gracious and loving to other women's children. She showed me that a woman could step up and fill a void left by another woman and do it simply because it was the right thing to do.

Glenda the Good Witch

I don't know how old I was when I first saw *The Wizard of Oz*, but I recognized that mean witch right away! I had already met females like her in my short life. It was Glenda the Good

Witch who came as a surprise. Such a

beautiful, joyful human being existed!

I wanted her to be my mommy so

bad. When she spoke, her voice was

the sound of sunshine to me. I

physically ached with longing for

Glenda the Good Witch to be my

mommy. Even as an adult, when I

watch *The Wizard of Oz,* I remember the

longing, and am still a little bit sad she

wasn't my mommy.

Before Glenda the Good Witch all

women were wicked witches.   Glenda

gave me hope that other types of mothers might exist.

Today people say when I'm particularly happy, mixed with silly, my voice sounds like it's just about to break into laughter. I believe long ago, a sparkling ray from Glenda the Good Witch shot out of the television and I swallowed it.

She Who Held my Secrets

At age thirty-three I made a major life change and got clean and sober. My old way of living would have put me in a very early grave, but somehow, I felt there was something worth saving in me.

I met with like-minded people and one day, after a meeting, I didn't immediately scamper away. I was standing on the clubhouse porch as a blonde woman was tagging people on the shoulder, saying, "You're coming over, and you're coming over, and you, and you." She was tapping everyone and she tapped me too!

Despite having no idea where she lived and not having a car, I soon found myself at her house. It was filled to the brim with laughing, smiling people. I wasn't laughing or smiling much in those days so I wriggled into a corner, sat cross-legged on the floor, and took in the scene. It was a pretty impressive sight.

As I sat there, letting the laughter wash over me, I got to thinking about what I had heard earlier. In order to stay off drugs, I needed to find someone to work with me and to show me what had already been shown to them. They called it "A New Way of Living". I was told to look for someone who had what I wanted. As I looked at the happy laughing people in her home, I decided she could be my Secret Keeper. I just had to get the courage to ask her.

It took me a while but I did end up asking her. I'll never forget the look on her face as she responded with "I would be honored!". I was a homeless drug addict, been in jail, and not seen my children in months.   Honored? That was the last word I expected to come out of her mouth!

We worked together for the next six years, and in time, I understood why she said honored. She knew all my secrets and it didn't affect her opinion of me. She actually loved me more!

We went through my life story and she taught me how to be a responsible adult. The healing process, letting go of emotional pain and believing I am enough, began with her guidance. I am grateful for the lessons in acceptance I learned from her. Now I have the privilege of saying, "I would be honored" to others.

My Favorite Landlady

If I wanted to stay off drugs, I had to stop sleeping on a drug dealer's couch. So, at 10 days clean I landed a job and started looking for a new place to live. It had to be cheap, really cheap.

I looked in the paper for studios. Those

got snapped up quickly! I looked on the

bulletin board at the clubhouse.

Nothing. Reluctantly I turned to the

rooms-for-rent section of the

newspaper.

Renting a room was my least

desired option but I was going to any

lengths to stay clean. If I had to live in a

stranger's house to get off that drug

dealer's couch, so be it!   I was going to

rent a room. I spotted a place, within

budget, with the extra bonus of utilities

included. When I went to look at the

place, I met the woman I lovingly call My Favorite Landlady.

She asked me if I had a job. I exuberantly replied "Yes!" She asked how long I had worked there. "Less than a month" I answered. Then she asked where had I worked before that.

I knew an honest answer could lose me this place but I had promised to stop lying. I hung my head and said "I haven't had a job in three years". Her silence caused me to raise my head and I saw her looking at me with a twinkle in her eye as she asked "Are you in recovery?" "Yes!" exploded out

of my mouth. "Oh honey," she said,
"you're in the right place".

That peaceful haven is where I laid
my head for the next year. It was a
stable address to begin regular
visitation with my children and I had
permission to go into her house and eat
anything in the fridge. She said she
always made too much food. (It took
me a couple years to figure out she
made extra food so I'd have something
to eat.)

My Favorite Landlady taught me
that I could pay bills on time, respect
her home and keep a job. Ultimately,

she showed me that I am lovable by loving me without conditions. I hope she's done traveling soon so I can put a copy of this book in her hands and thank her for trusting an addict with only a few days clean.

I used to say that I'm a motherless child, but life has shown me I have had many mothers all along the way. Now, I understand each woman did the best she could considering her skills and circumstances and I value the lessons each one taught me. They have all helped shape me into the beautiful, sassy, powerful crone I am today.

Today, I mother myself. I'm a pretty good mom and I'm proud of how I look after myself.

Permission to nurture: GRANTED

"You own everything that happened to you. Tell your stories. If people wanted you to write warmly about them, they should have behaved better."

Anne Lamott

2
PARENTS

In 1979 I was raped by a masked stranger who woke me out of my sleep with a hand across my mouth and a knife at my throat. I was 16.

At this time in the South, all 16-year-old females were virgins. I wasn't and the rape kit revealed two types of semen in my body. This made the evidence unusable. The disgust of the hospital staff and police was palpable. When the rape kit results were revealed to my parents, they said it was just a boy from school and told me I was a whore.

It seemed apparent to me that they would have preferred my first sexual experience to have been at knifepoint. They offered me two choices; stay in the South and live in a reform school until eighteen, or live with relatives in California. I chose California.

California was beautiful. The atmosphere of equality contrasted strongly compared to the South. I well remember my surprise at seeing a couple, one white, one black, holding hands. I hope I didn't stare. Stifling, antiquated ideas, would not go far in California!

Soon after I moved in with my relatives, letters started arriving from my parents. My relatives would read them then hide them. I did ask to read the letters too, but they knew it would be too painful for me.

The letters were filled with photos of me. I was being purged from the family photo albums; the evidence of my existence tossed away. I cried the tears of an abandoned and wounded child, unworthy of love or inclusion.

The next fifteen years were years of silence. The relatives who took me in grew elderly. One died and one was placed in residential care. At this point all letters from the South stopped.

I moved on with my California life. I married, had children, divorced, attended church, did drugs, had therapy, and quit drugs. Now clean and sober I got in touch with my family.

We had a bit of a honeymoon period, prodigal daughter and all, but eventually, the weekly calls became harder and harder for me to make. While both parents were loving and forgiving, over time I became aware that I had been cast permanently as the bad girl made good.

Over the years, a truce evolved between myself and Parent A. Parent A even took some ownership for acts of physical and emotional abuse. In contrast, Parent B remained silent, enjoying the communication and relationship, but letting the other parent bear all the blame for the actions they had taken together. The phone calls, now monthly, filled me with dread because by the time I hung up I felt completely fake and shattered.

I began to question myself. What was behind these feelings? How is a responsible, beloved and powerful woman reduced to this by a single phone call? After a long period of reflection and prayer, the answer came. Parent B had never taken responsibility for complicity.

At sixteen, Parent B told me I was a whore and said the rapist was probably a friend of mine who broke into the house where I was staying*.

*I was not welcome in my parents' home. The rapist, The Southwest Molester, was caught and sentenced to an 830-year sentence, served consecutively for crimes against eighteen females. He died in prison of COVID-19 on September 9, 2020.

Years later, Parent A apologized for treating a rape victim in this way, but Parent B had not. In fact, Parent B had never asked for my side of things, didn't seem to see anything wrong with treating a rape victim this way, and never acknowledged it was a serial

rapist and not some high school boy.

After months of contemplation,

prayer and long talks with close friends,

I wrote my parents. My goal was to

open a dialogue and make room for

honest communication. That's not what

happened. Instead of clear ground for a

new start I got a letter full of vitriol like

those from 1979-80.

The letter was a poison arrow

which hit the bullseye of my heart.   It

caused so much despair and confusion.

I felt like a huge axe had split my brain

and my body into two distinct halves "before the letter" and "after the letter".

It was abundantly clear that we'd made exactly no progress whatsoever. Under the surface they still saw me as an incorrigible teen. Again, I was not welcome.   They could not give me the understanding I desired. How could I protect myself?

Then I had a wild thought! I could shut the door on my parents! My mind raced! Such drastic behavior! They brought me into this world -- it's just not done! Unless I do it.

Who could give me permission to shut the door on my parents?

I could!

And so, I did.

Permission to be respected: GRANTED

My permissions

"A college education is one of the few purchases a person can make that cannot be repossessed or auctioned off"

Ken Ilunga's

3
COLLEGE

When I turned eighteen in 1980 there was no mention of my starting college or continuing to live where I was. Getting married seemed my only choice. So, I married another immature adult and went to work full-time.

My husband had a video arcade addiction and irregular employment, so our money needed to s-t-r-e-t-c-h. For a while he went to junior college but his arcade addiction soon canceled his class attendance. I continued to work full-time to support us and the arcade.

Fast forward to 1990, when I quit my crappy job and started junior college myself. As a divorced mom living in subsidized housing with two kids, I was eligible for many grants. That first semester I made the Dean's List! In the second semester I end up with F's and was homeless in six months. How could this be? In one word: Methamphetamine.

By 1993 my addiction was full blown and had I lost custody of my children temporarily. Then things got worse. In January 1994, a house rented in my name was busted by the DEA. The guy who split my lip, and who I then split-up with, had been dealing drugs from that address. He was finally caught and served a year in jail. I was charged as an accomplice and also went to jail.

My ninety-day sentence was commuted down to sixty days for good behavior. (Of course, I behaved well, jail was terrifying!) I also lost custody of the kids permanently but was allowed visitation.

Upon my release, I had no plan and was back on drugs in no time. My promises meant nothing to me. I broke them all the time. Visits with the kids were irregular. Suddenly, out of the blue, I was struck by the consequences of my choices and their effects on my loved ones. Having had this realization, which I call a spiritual awakening, I quit drugs for good.

Now clean and sober, I sorted donated clothes for $4.65 an hour while remembering the college opportunity I had swapped for drugs. That opportunity was gone for good! I told myself I'd had my chance. Besides, who was I to think that after all I'd done, and thirty-three years old to boot, I could start the long process to become a licensed marriage and family therapist?

I continued to tell myself this for the next three years. I only had fourteen units of junior college credit. It was a long way from a Bachelor's, never mind a Master's degree, providing 3,000 hours supervised therapy, and two exhaustive exams. So, I set my sights on a certificate program in 1999. I'd lost the chance I had for a college degree.

In 2001, I began working with drug-addicted survivors of intimate partner violence as a certified alcohol and drug counselor. I loved my job and felt I was at last comfortably settled. Then, after a year-and a-half, I was let go from the job I loved.

"How was the decision made to let me go instead of other people in my department?" I asked. The boss answered, "We kept the people with college degrees". At that moment I vowed to myself this would never happen to me again.

Fifteen years after my first thrown-away opportunity to return to college, I earned a bachelor's degree. It was 2005, I was 43 years old and had been clean and sober for ten years. I continued my sobriety and became a licensed marriage and family therapist in 2011.

Permission to get educated: GRANTED

"We destroy ourselves when we stop feeling. If you bury your feelings within you, you become a graveyard."—Bernie S. Siegal

4

FEELINGS

Can you feel and identify your feelings? I had a difficult time feeling anything. It was painful, and produced anxiety in me. The anxiety went underground so I couldn't find the bulb of feeling: I couldn't backtrack and find the origin of the discomfort.

At that time, I had no gardening tools to help me till the ground of my internal desert. I just hoped sugar or food or speed or alcohol would help me avoid the packed, parched terrain of my consciousness. Or at least knock it out so it wouldn't bother me anymore.

This has given me years of challenges. The first challenge is dessert. As a young girl I stole desserts when I babysat. At home I stole money out of bureau drawers for desserts. I snuck extra helpings of desserts. I would eat all the desserts I could find, rooting through cupboards and freezers to find the treasures within.

I was eight years old when "Willy Wonka and the Chocolate Factory" came out. It was a visual of which to dream. Holidays, for me, were summed up by the particular treat assigned: Valentines' Day, chocolate; Easter, candy eggs and marshmallow bunnies; Fourth of July, red, white, blue frosted cupcakes, Jell-O molds, and jelly beans; Halloween, lots and lots of really good candy; Thanksgiving, pumpkin pie with extra whipped cream; Christmas, fudge, peppermint sticks, and cookies. My year was a revolving calendar of treats.

I don't remember ever feeling like I had enough candy. Once I began experimenting with marijuana, I loved the munchies. I now had a good reason to eat the sweet snacks provided by friends to celebrate our highs. But, weed and I parted ways because when I got high and ate, I fell asleep. That wasn't fun so I swapped the sugar from sweets to the sugar the body creates when it metabolizes alcohol.

I short circuited when the bottle was empty, the bar closed, I'd thrown up everything, or the room spun when I lay down. I later learned throwing up meant I had a fatal amount of alcohol in my blood. Throwing up had saved me from alcohol poisoning.

When I moved to California for a fresh start at age 16, I stuck to only cigarettes for a while. Married at eighteen, pregnant at 20, I again turned to sugary treats and fast food. I had cravings don't you know! The baby wanted fast food and candy bars and I put on at least an extra 50 pounds with my first pregnancy.

A few years later I moved next-door to a family whose primary breadwinner was a truck driver. The driver's spouse introduced me to methamphetamine. We would do lines of crank, as it was called then, clean our houses, bake cupcakes, and talk, talk, talk. We did this a couple times a week and I lost the weight I had put on.

Too proud to go on any kind of financial assistance, I worked the night shift in a chicken processing factory. My home was spotless, laundry folded, closets organized. With a full-time job and a two-year-old, I was able to stay on top of everything! This was the early 80s when feminism was in the "I am woman, I do it all" stage. So, I did, as did many others.

Speed was everywhere. Doctors prescribed women little pink pills to lose weight.

Later on, when I switched to powdered speed, just one line in the morning would keep me going all day, and I slept almost every night. Over time, I became a daily user.

One hundred dollars a week wasn't very difficult to earn as my other living expenses were low, especially my grocery budget! When my next-door neighbors moved away, I found another supplier. The cost of my supply dropped substantially when I started joining the new drug-dealing couple in bed. However, this ended abruptly when one of them came to my home professing undying love for me.

Around this time, I went out to drinks with friends who needed a fourth person in the party. Their friend was a tall, blonde, blue-eyed human with a lovely smile. This human could be my ticket out of that drug infected town! But before we moved to Southern California, I spent all night sanding a table, without gloves, while on methamphetamine.

Having had that painful lesson, I didn't use meth for four years after the move. Alcohol did the job. It killed my anxiety and was easier to use because it is legal. I broke no laws walking into the liquor store and purchasing my preferred flavor then walking home to drink it. Besides, alcohol is socially accepted and I drank socially, in that, I drank with other people who were drinking.

My flavor was Gallo wine by the gallon. A gallon kept me supplied for a couple days. I caught a buzz fairly quickly but was able to keep my wits about me until the children were put to bed. The children were young enough to stay where I put them, which helped immensely. I had worked all day, cooked, fed, helped with homework, bathed the children. A good buzz was no less than I deserved!

Flash forward and I've graduated to Seagram's VO with ginger ale. I'm living alone with the children. I can no longer blame my drinking on a co-drinker. It's evening, the house is quiet, and I am standing in front of the open refrigerator, looking at the liter of ginger ale.

A thought pops in my head sideways -- I'm drinking for no reason. There is no co-drinker in this house; it's all me. I can remember shaking my head a bit, trying to dislodge the thought. My brain suddenly refused entrance to thoughts that had previously justified my drinking. There, in front of the fridge, with no one but myself, I had a decision to make. I squared my shoulders, took a deep breath, and asked myself, "Well?".

I intuitively knew that stopping for me meant stopping completely. So, I let go of alcohol as a coping mechanism and trusted that I would find other ways to deal with life. I trusted I would be taught to fly, and I was. But the day came when I was presented with a line of methamphetamine on a mirror. I did it without hesitation.

I managed to convince myself that I had fallen in love with a drug dealer, and in this way was able to believe that I wasn't exchanging sex for drugs. It was a good time, or so I thought, until that boyfriend gave me a split lip. I left him and ended up living in my car and couch surfing when the law caught up to me. I ended up doing time for being under the influence of a controlled substance. The party was over. Jail was no joke.

I quit using, threw away my paraphernalia, and set about making some new friends. These new friends taught me how to live without using drugs. Once I wasn't using drugs or alcohol to nub my feelings my sweet tooth came back like a three-year-old at a birthday party!

I gained weight; first ten pounds, then 20, 30, and finally 50 pounds. I blamed my hectic schedule. I blamed the coworkers who shared their sugar bounty as it found my booty. I blamed holidays. I blamed people who filled the cupboards with desirable sugary foods. I blamed grocery stores for the two-for-one sales. The person I didn't blame was myself. It took me a long time to realize that I was the common denominator.

I chose hours of television over walking. I chose eating out over cooking at home. I chose to make a pint of ice cream a single serving. I chose to spend two dollars on a soda and candy bar instead of a half-pound of grapes. I chose to avoid difficult conversations and ate instead.

I was rudely awakened from the food coma when, lying on my bed, I was unable to zip my size 18 pants. That was it! I refused to purchase anything size 20. So began years of trying different diets: cabbage soup; lemon cayenne water; water fasting; South Beach; Atkins; Keto; Paleo; vegetarian; and vegan. Every single one of these diets made me grumpy.

The results were great for a period of time, depending on my will-power and stubbornness. However, underneath it all, I continued to feel.

I felt ugly. I felt like an outsider in my own life. I felt envy. I felt like a failure. *I felt, felt, felt, so I ate, ate, ate.*

I began working on the "Why's" behind my addictive behaviors. The weight gain kept me from being noticed and let me escape my feeling just as drugs and alcohol had. Once I accepted it would be safe to be seen and to feel I started making lifestyle changes.

Today I have a BMI the chart says is normal. Most days I walk my exuberant puppy. Some days we walk for 20 minutes, some days we walk for an hour. The food I eat grows in soil and is harvested, not developed in a lab and made in a factory. Only Willy Wonka's Factory has a cookie tree!

Now, I have given myself permission to be seen and to feel. It is important to me to always remember how much of my life was consumed by consumption -- be it sugar, food, drugs or booze – and how unrewarding that life was.

Today I talk about my feelings and no longer try to solve every problem on my own. I care about my health and my body too much to allow an uncomfortable feeling put me back on the road to self-destruction.

Permission to Feel: GRANTED

My permissions

:The first step to getting what you want

is to have the courage to get rid of what

you don't."

Zig Ziglar

5
CAR

My first car was a 1966 Dodge Coronet 500. While I was learning to drive on a permit, I snuck the keys and went for a joy ride through the cemetery where I was sure not to run into another car. I sideswiped a wall on the way in and scratched the entire length of the car. Then I drove it home and parked it so the scratch couldn't be noticed from the house. There's a scene in *Ferris Bueller's Day Off* that reminds me of this.

I was promptly caught by my parents who were rightfully indignant at my attempts to avoid punishment. They were very angry! I'm sure I lost car privileges for a period of time, but what really lasted was the belief, "I don't deserve a nice car".

I drove a series of dented, rusted cars, vehicles missing hub caps, and in need of paint, until 2002 when I finally bought my first new car. It was the most basic model on the lot with a standard transmission and no sound system. But, before I made the first payment, my job laid me off. Somehow each payment got made while I lived carefully on unemployment benefits until I found another job.

The commute to the new job took two hours a day and I was grateful to have a new and reliable car for the drive.   However, the miles accumulated very quickly and the two-hour commute was hard on my body. I needed luxury. But luxury eluded me because, don't you know, I had a nice car once and I snuck it out and damaged it. I didn't deserve a nice car!

That commute and that car lasted two more years. Then, my sweetheart at the time suggested a fancier car with more features might make the drive more palatable. After this suggestion, I test drove any and all cars I thought I might like, finally settling on a convertible. What other car could I possibly want to drive two hours a day, up and down the coast of sunny California? It was a beautiful car with an amazing sound system. The moment

I sat in it, I wanted it so badly it wrenched my heart.

My heart wrenched because, as I sat in this beautiful car, I remembered, "I don't deserve a nice car". So, I took the car back to the dealer and walked away from the enticing offer on the table. On the way home, my sweetie asked me why I walked away from such an amazing deal. I told the story of the Dodge that had taken place twenty-five years earlier.

Saying it out loud helped me see that I was carrying an old worn-out story whose time had passed. We turned around and drove back to the dealership. The salesperson was with another buyer. We waited. After some time, the salesperson took us into the office, sat us down and said the earlier offer was rescinded. Now the cost of the car was very close to the sticker price and outside of my car budget. Stunned, we walked away from my dream car. "I don't deserve a nice car" became even more deeply rooted in my subconscious and I went home defeated. My dreams and desires were dead like road kill.

The following weekend my
sweetie dragged my hopeless,
dreamless body to another dealership
selling my dream car. We went in and
the previous experience, which I wore
all over my face, was explained to the
salesperson. After another test drive, I
was struggling to find a way to give
myself permission to have a nice car. I
felt my chance had gone away and I
struggled to dream again. The manager
asked me to write down the amount I
would pay for the car. I rounded up the
number offered by the previous

salesperson. The manager glanced at the number and said, "I can do that".

As I drove off the lot, in my limited-edition convertible, tears of gratitude flowed from my eyes. I said over and over, "I can have what I want, I can have what I want. Thank you. Thank you. Thank you."

Permission to have Comfort: GRANTED

My permissions

"FAMILY ISN'T ALWAYS BLOOD. IT'S THE PEOPLE IN YOUR LIFE WHO WANT YOU IN THEIRS; THE ONES WHO ACCEPT YOU AS YOU ARE. THE ONES WHO WOULD DO ANYTHING TO SEE YOU SMILE AND WHO LOVE YOU NO MATTER WHAT."

ANONYMOUS

6

SIBLINGS

Like many modern American

families, I have siblings cast across the

United States. We share drops of blood

and some genetic code but those are

the only common denominators

between me and them. Over the years

we have tried to get and stay connected

without any real success.

In my teenage years I tried to

connect with my older sibling in

California. He had been adopted by a

family who deeply loved him. I yearned

to reconnect with the brother who left

my life before I turned three but he

rarely returned my calls. My younger

brother, who I only found out about

when I was 17, was also raised in

adoptive family who deeply loved him.

Over the years, one of us three would

attempt a reunion and try to have

regular phone calls, but often the calls were left unanswered and messages were not returned.

My two southern siblings are a more than a decade younger than me. Small children under five when I moved out, they have few memories of time spent with me. On my rare return visits, they would put in an appearance and treat me lovingly. However, the substance of our relationship wasn't strong enough to survive when I wasn't there in the flesh.

I didn't do a good job of keeping in touch with them when they were younger, as I was going through my own difficulties. They also aroused feelings of jealousy in me. I could so easily see the love my parents had for them and they were not subjected to the "you're worthless" treatment that I had endured.

Between us siblings it has been a wretched round-robin of refusal and rejection. My jealousy and envy prevented me from connecting deeply with any of them. I was carrying around the dangerous "if only I'd been loved like you were" feeling and it tainted my dealings with all of them.

The truth is, it is tiring to always be the one reaching out into empty air, and natural to feel hurt by non-responsive attempts at relationship. So, it was easy for each of us to abandon the unrequited efforts in favor of situations that bore fruit. We got from others what we couldn't get from blood relations.

We are all over forty, and it doesn't appear that there will be a different ending to this story. They have families of their own now and I'm sure they are happy and loved in their lives, as am I.

I wish I could tell you that we did eventually find a way to make strong connections, but we didn't. The trick to accepting the situation, and giving myself permission to leave them alone, is knowing that we all gave what we could when we could.

Sometimes a happy ending eludes us. Sometimes, that happy ending starts and stops like a new driver working out the particulars of a manual transmission. Sure enough, some people figure out the pedal coordination and drive just fine, but some people don't. Their feet are not able to do the pedal dance, and, after stalling out every stop sign, they give up and drive an automatic.

Like that new driver, I had no instructions for the pedal dance and no music to go with it. There was no map telling me how to connect.

There are many stories about heart connections made after decades of absence, but I'm here to tell you that if your happy ending doesn't come, eventually it'll be all right.

Permission to let go: GRANTED

"Your present circumstances don't determine where you can go, they merely determine where you start."

Nido Qubein

7
MENTAL HEALTH

"Poor little Susie what shall we do? Put her in the corner until she turns blue!" I don't know when I first heard those words but considering the deep cut through my brain, I must've heard them a lot. It was my parents sarcastic to response to my deep sadness.

I've come to believe I was depressed from a very early age. My grandfather told me Incubator Mom left me in my crib for hours. She left my life before my second birthday. When my father was drafted into the Vietnam War my older brother was adopted into another family and I was left with Pushy Scary Mom.

It was almost two years before my dad got a compassionate discharge from the Army. When he came back, I was four years old. He met and married Off to a Bad Start Mom and the three of us drove from California to the South.

During the long drive across the country, with two near strangers, I had constant diarrhea. It was probably anxiety. In my short life changes hadn't exactly been positive and life affirming. I imagine I was terrified. My parents wouldn't have known or even thought about anxiety or depression.

Back then psychology was in its infancy and child psychology was still in the womb. Recently I found a YouTube video showing an emotionally deprived baby filmed in the late 50's. The baby lays on its back, staring at its hand, seemingly unaware of the camera. It's a heartbreaking video to watch: Those eyes haunt me. The feelings of that baby strike home in my heart.

Another YouTube video by John Bowlby, an early pioneer in child psychology, called *A Two-Year-Old Goes to the Hospital*, records a little girl as she deals with her separation from her parents. I wondered as I watched it, did I react similarly? After all I had lost my mother, brother and father in less than a year.

Child psychology was so new no one considered I might have been exhibiting symptoms of a disorder.

Decades later, Off to a Bad Start mom told me that I would shove a book at her and say in a menacing tone, "Read to me". She didn't know why I was alternating between anger and sadness so much. She thought I didn't like her.

The frustration this newlywed, instant-mother felt ended up expressed on my legs. In those days it wasn't child abuse to raise welts on legs. Meanwhile, my father sat quietly in his chair trying be absolved for coming to this marriage with a child, the evidence of his loving another woman.

I escaped to my bed whenever I could and was almost impossible to rouse. A new day was to be postponed as long as possible. This earned me the title of lazy. I remember wandering the street about age eight, stopping to ask the neighbor three doors down, "Do you need a little girl?" "No honey," he said, "Where are your parents?".

By age 13 I started running away from home. Off and on I went into foster care and group homes. The appointed family therapist said in an exasperated tone, "Our goal is to get Susan back in the home!". My parents responded with, "We don't want her back home". During an individual session, the therapist unguardedly said to me, "It's a wonder you are not crazy".

I was plagued by chronic insomnia. I lay awake for hours only to be woken up after a few hours of sleep and told to complete chores. There was nothing gentle in this waking. The lights were flipped on, the covers pulled off me and the shouting -- berating me for my lazy imperfection – began.

In my 20's, I took pride in the fact that I survived it all without going crazy.

I definitely considered myself defective -- scared of the dark, panicking in crowds, insomnia, dragging my tired heavy body through the day -- but not crazy!

On the outside I smiled at my children as we decorated our home with a butcher paper and crayon mural. We recorded funny answering machine messages. We had adventures with a dollar each that often ended with us at the ice cream counter in the drugstore. Speed helped me keep up with my young children.

With grace and 15 years of sobriety I reached my 40's. I'm at work screening potential clients for entry into a pilot mental health program. The criteria: a mental health diagnosis, a substance use disorder and the commitment of a crime. I discover nearly all of the clients have a trauma history. During the interview process I ask them if they have experienced the textbook criteria for a mental health diagnosis. They tell me what the text book criteria look like in their lives and I began to recognize traits of my own.

So, I found a psychiatrist who asked me those same trauma history questions. The official diagnosis came back as depression, anxiety, and PTSD. Three of them! It was a blow to my pride. But I started taking my medication, started sleeping all night, and began waking up rested.

Now my days begin with a smile and pep in my step. I've tripped over the diagnoses a couple of times as I worked my way through the *Permissions*. Today, I consider myself mostly in remission. I can get flareups around anniversaries or holidays but I know how to wade through and keep my head above water.

Mental health diagnoses are just the language helpers use to steer us to the help needed. I no longer feel anxious, depressed or reactive most of the time because I take my medicine. Having the diagnoses of depression, anxiety, and Post Traumatic Stress Response, (let's get the disorder out of it), means I can get treatment.

Permission to take meds: Granted

"Leap and the Net will Appear"

John Burroughs

8
LEAP

I was pretty good at checking out of life. Until I was 13, I checked out by spending all the time I could reading books. I enjoyed letting myself be transported to some other world. I'd get so immersed I didn't hear the first calls to dinner, chore time, or errands. Reluctantly, I'd leave the book world and re-enter my life making sure to leave a small part of my brain in the book for daydreaming. I found other ways to check out discussed earlier in this book so let's talk about checking in.

When I got off drugs and alcohol I began experimenting with the belief "Leap and the net will appear". Life shifted. It wasn't easy to leap at first. Negative self-talk blasted its opinion at full volume: WHAT? Who do you think you are? What makes you think YOU can? What makes you think YOU deserve …! "Slowly, over time I came to believe the net would appear.

Could I raise my children on eight dollars an hour? The net appeared. I absolutely could. When I lost my dream job years later, the net was there. When I lost both my home and my partner the net was there. Both times I went on disability the net was there. Gradually, I learned to trust the net would appear when the rug was pulled out from under my feet.

If I sincerely believed this statement to be true, perhaps I could make the leaps I wanted. So, I practiced expanding my belief in "Leap and the Net will Appear". I quit a union job in public service to start my own private practice. The net was there! I gave up my cozy cottage in the country and moved in with my lover and then, suddenly, I moved out. Miraculously, my country cottage was still available! The net was there! I found I could choose to leap and a net would appear.

I have also used this saying to take the risks involved in having adventures. I leapt on a plane to Hawaii and played in a warm ocean. I leapt into my friend's car and drove across the upper United States believing the new job I'd just started would still be there for me when I got back. It was. The net was there. I took a huge leap and moved to New Zealand for a year!

Most recently, knowing the net would be there, I stood strong to practically everyone important to me when I decided to move back to the partner I had run from. Right now, at this very moment, I believe in the net as I write my story to share with you.

Permission to Leap: GRANTED

"A true relationship is two imperfect

people refusing to up on each other."

anonymous

9
SELF

One of my most difficult therapy sessions featured adult me and four-year-old me. I was supposed to bond with this younger me. "No," I told my therapist, "I don't want to go near her." "Why?" asked my therapist. "Because she's ugly, and smelly, her hair is all matted up, and I don't think she's had a

bath in quite a while!". My therapist
suggested I move toward her. "NO
WAY, I don't want that stink on me!".

I could barely look at four-year-old
me. Smelly, with matted hair and
grime-caked skin, she looked like
something out of a *Raised by Wolves*
scene. I recoiled at the idea of bringing
her close to me. Somehow my
therapist was able to get me to engage
that four-year-old, and suddenly I was
hugging her, crying, sobbing, and
wailing.

Next thing I knew she was in a tub
full of bubbles and I was washing her

hair, scrubbing her skin, and gently brushing the tangles out of her hair. I put lotion and powder on her and put her in a clean flannel nightgown. When I reached down to hold her close -- Pop! She became part of me and was no longer separate.

My childhood memories are mostly triggered by looking at photographs. I wasn't a child for long. I was smoking cigarettes by age thirteen, smoking pot soon after, and drinking alcohol soon after that. I used for effect from the very start. Substances lowered my inhibitions.

I don't think I had sober sex until I was married. In the South, during the 70s, there were two genders; male and female, and one kind of coupling, a boy and a girl. Outside of an isolated alcohol infused experiment with a high school chum, I only had sex with boys. In the 80s I dated only men, but in the late 90s there was a change.

She had long hair, the color of wheat, and hazel eyes. We met through mutual friends and started hanging out. We took turns cooking for each other, enjoyed long drives, hiking, and going to the beach. At one point I suggested we end the friendship because I felt she was getting attached and I would only break her heart because I wasn't a lesbian. But the friendship didn't end.

We were sitting in restaurant when we began to hold hands. Then an ice cube slid very slowly across first her hand, then mine, leaving a trail of cool water. The restaurant grew warmer and warmer.

A few days later I was driving home from work when I realized I was hoping there would be a message from her on the answering machine. Almost simultaneously, an awareness flooded me. I felt like I did when I was hoping for a phone call from a male crush. OMG, I had a crush on a female! I went home, saw the blinking light and called her to tell her what I'd just realized.

Shortly after, she walked in my house, stepped up to me, and a hug turned into a hold. Time stopped. We became one being. Unfortunately, we were going in opposing directions and the relationship ended after a few years.

I thoroughly expected to return to dating men after this relationship. I wasn't really a lesbian! I just happened to accidentally fall in love with a woman who drove a delivery truck, could build things and used tools: So not really a woman type woman at all, I told myself. Imagine my surprise when I had feelings for another woman!

I was still a single mother of two children. I clearly had relations with men! But relationships with men didn't feel the same. A relationship with a man was no emotional burden at all. I pretty quickly moved on to the next. I didn't understand why my friends would spend weeks crying over some guy. But that first break up with a woman? That shredded my heart.

Girlfriend number two was also good at home repairs, initiated most of our sex, and wore fairly androgynous clothing. I wore the same. As I accepted my lesbian identity my clothes simplified to button down blouses and pants. My feet were encased in clunky earth-tone shoes, and since my toes were rarely uncovered, I didn't wear polish. The lesbians I knew looked like that, so I did too. I wanted to be in the club and to fit in.

Then the rules changed. My she wanted to be he. "OK," I said, "I've been with men more of my life than women, and I love you, so love will prevail." That's not what happened.

She started binding her breasts to make them less noticeable and cut off her beautiful chestnut curls. In the hardware store, as her gender became more difficult to discern, it was me who would offer the assist. "I think he wants the stainless steel." As his gender became recognizable, I disappeared. I became the spouse, ignored and pushed aside. The man was now in charge. I didn't like that one bit. I wasn't a wife and I didn't want to give up my gay card.

I continued to stand by him, as testosterone erased my girlfriend. There was now a man in my bed with hairy legs and a different body odor. He spent so much time in the mirror each evening looking for signs of facial hair that I started calling it "the nightly preening". He looked like a parrot pulling the keratin off of feathers.

I'll never forget those first moments after his top surgery, when they surgically removed breast tissue to create a masculine chest. In the recovery room, he opened his eyes in response to my voice and in an anesthesia-drunk voice sang, "Happy birthday to me, happy birthday to me". In that moment I understood how important this day truly was.

A few months after surgery he looked at me and said, "This isn't working is it?" I was relieved even as a part of me grieved. It took a while for me to get my bearings back after we split our household. I was disappointed in myself that I couldn't love the man in the way I had loved the woman.

In time I got to the place where I searched for my own identity. I let go of my preconceived notion of what a lesbian looks like. I asked myself what did I want to look like? I spent hours on a website a dear friend suggested to me and discovered there was actually a classification for my style and taste. I am a femme. Gone were the earth-tone shoes and blouses: I returned to the heels, dresses, perfume and lipstick that I love.

My preferred partner is a woman who is most comfortable in male clothing, with buzzed hair, who extends a hand to help me navigate terrain in heels. She's an old-school butch and a vanishing breed. As a femme, I am difficult to spot as a lesbian, unless I am in the company of my butch.

Despite the flak from some of my close blood relations, I am home. I fit my skin. I bake and my spouse cooks. I put together the flatpack furniture and do minor home repairs. Together, we share yard maintenance.

As gender and sexuality become less binary, space is created for every individual to be exactly who they are. Which is good, because according to Oscar Wilde, "Be yourself, everyone else is already taken".

Permission to be Me: GRANTED

"Life shrinks or expands in proportion to one's courage."

Anais Nin

10
LOVE

"I don't deserve love, because I am a bad person". This belief is sticky. Once it sets in, it takes some work to move it out. Work that is definitely not for the faint of heart.

I think loving is the most valuable tool we have for navigating this earth. Imagine the changes we will see when every imaginable situation has love applied. We would stop using our car horns and start using our turn signals. We would stop sending negative energy to other humans who are disrupting our day with their noise and intrusions. Parents with cranky children would receive smiles and compassion from others. People wearing a long day on their face might be allowed cuts in line or have doors opened for them. "After you," two words that evoke kindness. Ah, what a world! It brings to mind Louis Armstrong's song. But guess what I discovered?

I can't give what I don't have. So, if I don't love me, I can't love you.   And just how exactly do I love myself when I can cite chapter and verse as to why I should definitely not love myself?

After tuning into my own self-talk, I soon realized that when people in my life said nice things to me, about me, I immediately negated what they said. I did this by muttering comments to myself like "They don't know the inside of you" or "You're my friend, of course you'd say that". Any love that came to me I sent right back to where it came from. Pronto. No wonder I couldn't feel love. I blocked it neatly, completely,

and immediately!

To challenge and change this

mind-set I asked the Multiverse to show

me how others see me. A breakthrough

came when I was honored at an event.

I walked to the front of the room,

accepted my award, and stood still

while the crowd applauded. Frankly, I

wanted to rush my short speech and

get back to my seat as quickly as

possible, but I didn't. I stood there and

allowed myself to feel the energy that

rolled toward me. It was love. That

night I let it in.

So began the long, slow process of loving myself fully and completely. Lessons came in fits and starts. I'd make progress, feel better, and move on to something new. These complicated life lessons, for me, come in stages.

Like sunburnt skin, I work through layers, illuminate portions, and then I reach a place of needing to leave it alone as the fresh new skin heals. It has been fifteen or so years since that first breakthrough and I am still not done with this aspect of growth – of completely accepting and loving myself. I suspect there is no finish line or end date. In the meantime, I practice using some other tools.

I used to imagine my heart was dry and cracked from disuse. I began to imagine my heart as pink and pumping. The circulation of fresh blood and oxygen bringing me and my heart back to health. Sometimes, I also practice a heart opening. I place my fingers over my heart space and imagining energy flowing from my fingers into my heart. I breathe a measured inhale, hold, and exhale. Using this cycle of rhythmic breath helps me to feel calm and connected.

From here I can expand my feelings of gratitude.

Gratitude is a lovely way to open up my heart. I can feel gratitude at any moment simply by thinking of things that bring me joy: my loved ones; my home; my pet; my town; my life. As I think of what I'm grateful for, I say them out loud. "I am grateful for the sun because the light and warmth provide for life. I'm grateful for the love I'm shown by my pet" and so on.

Occasionally, I'll imagine the very air around me as full of love from the Multiverse and the Earth. This love touches, and is absorbed by, the surface of my skin. As I draw the love in, I draw it up and out through my breath, my nose, my mouth and my eyes. I give love blasts out from my eyes to people who cross my path.

Often, when out walking with my dog, we become Super Susan and her super hero dog, Pupper Penny. Together our super power is love and we spread it everywhere and to everyone. Pupper Penny is a love-generating machine. On our daily walks she sends out so much love!

Eagerly, from the very end of her leash, with tail wagging, butt wiggling, and a smile on her face, she meets everyone with equal enthusiasm. The hurrying, well-dressed human gets the same enthusiasm as the homeless person.

Since Penny is part pit bull, sometimes people cross the street in order to avoid what they see as a dangerous dog. Since she gets so sad when she doesn't get to love-bomb, I've become her advocate. This opens me up to talking to strangers and connecting with folks I don't know.

Pupper Penny and her super power have taught me so much about love. I enjoy seeing the transformation on peoples' faces as she love-bombs them. Some of the love she spreads stays with folks throughout the day -- increasing the love each one of them has to spread -- like concentric ripples on the surface of water. Sometimes, I imagine the love expanding like floating soap bubbles passing from person to person, crossing new paths all day long.

People say that animals take on the personality of their owner and they are probably right most of the time. But not in my case. Pupper Penny has

made me a more loving and a more

social person. Our morning walks are

community service and a habit I deeply

treasure.

Permission to Love: GRANTED

"Everyone thinks of changing the world, but no one thinks of changing them self."

Leo Tolstoy

11

Endings Are Beginnings

We started this journey with me
getting my mug shot taken by the
police. Since then I have interviewed
drug addicted, homeless, criminals, and
socially isolated individuals. Their
stories of mental, physical, emotional,
and sexual abuse mirror my own

experiences. Since we have had similar experiences how is it that I survived and thrived? What is the difference?

Through a series of *Permissions,* I have allowed myself the freedom to let go of toxicity, feel with my whole heart, love unconditionally, nurture, get educated, and become self-employed. Along the way I also gifted myself with ending unhealthy relationships, a few adventures and some comfort. Now I sit here with degrees, licenses, a home, children, and grandchildren.

This small, short book landed with you for a reason. What do you need permission to do? End something? Start something? Finish something? My sincere wish is that you will gift yourself your own *Permissions* and take action. I'll be interested in hearing how it came out for you so send me an email and let me know what wonderful Permissions you have gifted yourself.

Permission to Change: GRANTED

ABOUT THE AUTHOR

Susan Utter lives in San Francisco with her beloved
Denise. They live a comfortable and simple life
surrounded by friends and fur babies. She can be reached
at fabfemme11@gmail.com and on YouTube
Fab_femme11